AF407540

Hex codes, or hexadecimal codes, are a way to represent colors in digital devices and web design. Each hex code refers to a very specific color. A hex color is expressed as a six-digit combination of numbers and letters, preceded by a pound sign or hashtag, defined by its mix of red, green, and blue (RGB). The first two letters or numbers refer to red, the next two refer to green, and the last two refer to blue.

The color values are defined as values between 00 and FF. Hex codes are a universal way to describe colors. This book is specifically about vegetable colors.

A is for arugula

A

#42603C

a is for asparagus

a

#87A96B

B is for beet

B

#8A1653

b is for broccoli

b

#76904B

C is for carrot

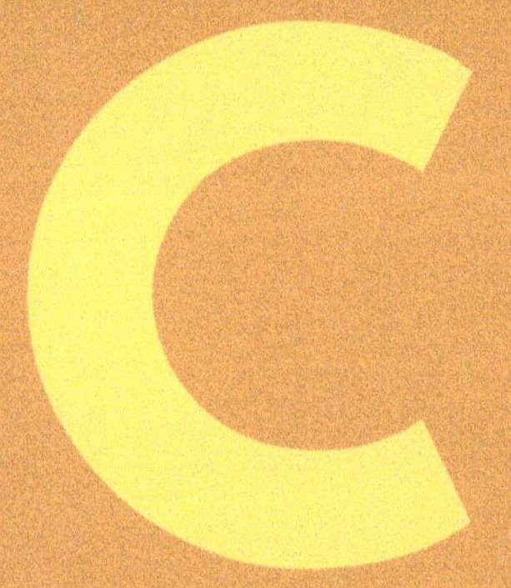

#ED9121

c is for corn

C

#FBEC5D

D is for daikon radish

D

#E2E8CF

d is for dill

d

#788D60

E is for edamame

E

#9CA389

e is for endive

e

#D7D182

F is for fava bean

F

#B9CF9C

f is for fennel

f

#D8C75F

G is for garbanzo bean

G

#EAD2AF

g is for garlic

#F2E9D2

H is for habanero

H

#CC554A

h is for horseradish

h

#EFE9DC

I is for iceberg lettuce

I

#CDE472

i is for idaho potato

#B79268

J is for jalapeño

J

#B1533C

j is for jicama

#F2DEBC

K is for kale

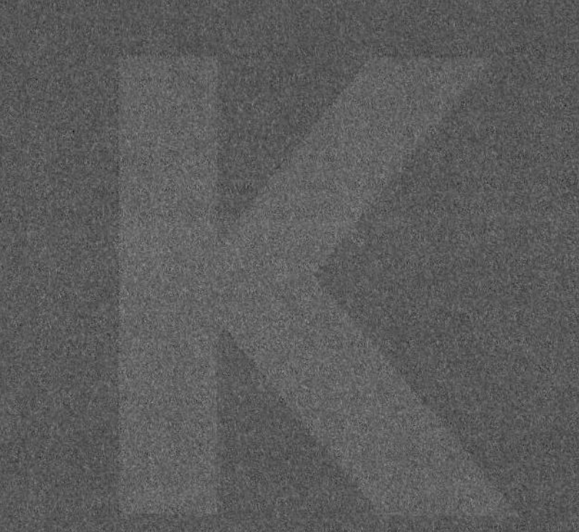

#38664C

k is for kidney bean

#9E6453

L is for lettuce

#94CF03

l is for lentil

l

#DCC8B0

M is for mung bean

M

#CAC76D

m is for mustard green

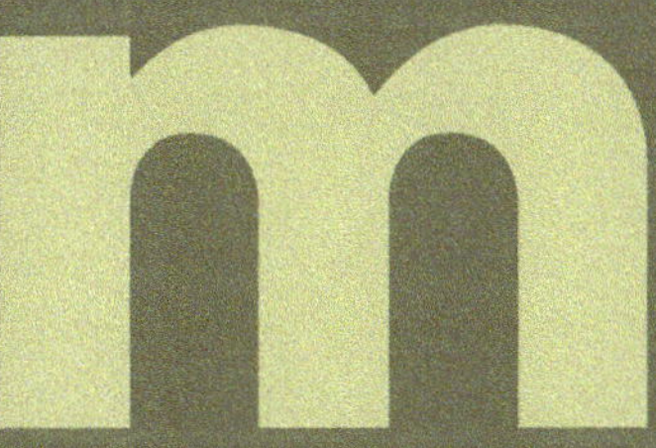

#6E6E30

N is for napa cabbage

N

#BEBB8D

n is for navy bean

n

#E8E4D8

O is for okra

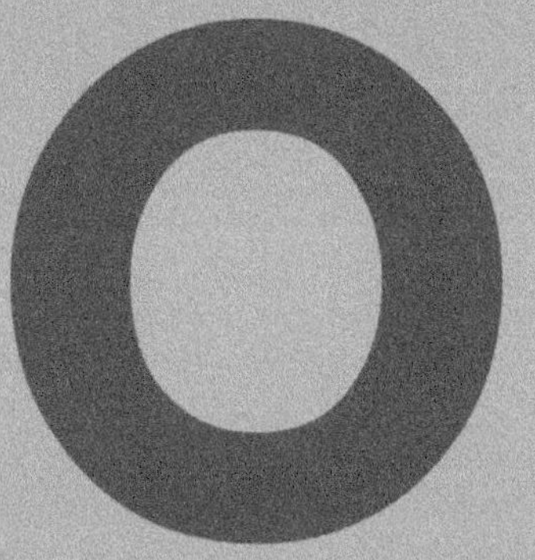

#5FA23E

o is for onion

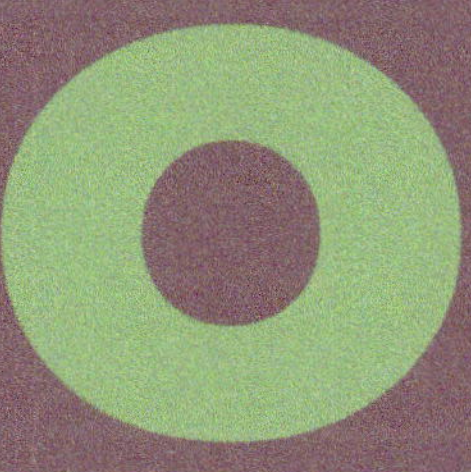

#894452

P is for pea

P

#8EAB12

p is for purple cabbage

p

#724C7B

Q is for quelite cenizo

#556B2C

q is for quelite mafafa

q

#728B1F

R is for radish

R

#A42E41

r is for rutabaga

r

#ECDDBE

S is for spinach

S

#3A683A

s is for spring onion

S

#AFD46D

T is for turmeric

T

#FE840E

t is for turnip

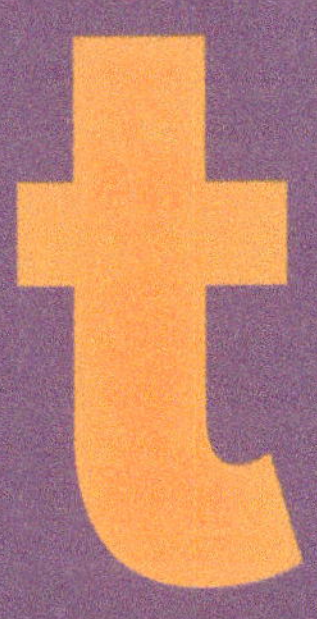

#975788

U is for urad bean

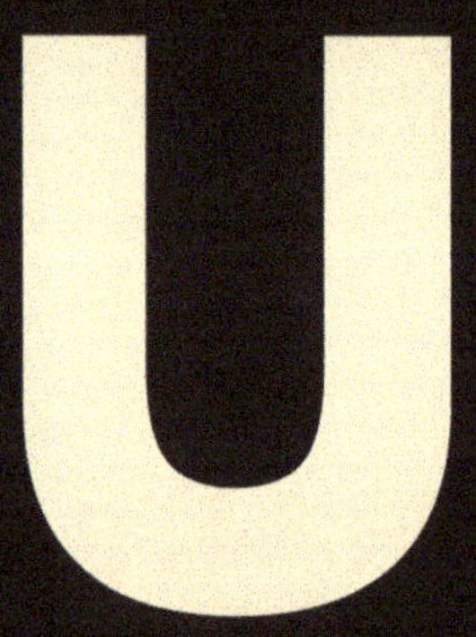

#1E1C18

u is for urad dal bean

U

#FFE9C0

V is for victoria rhubarb

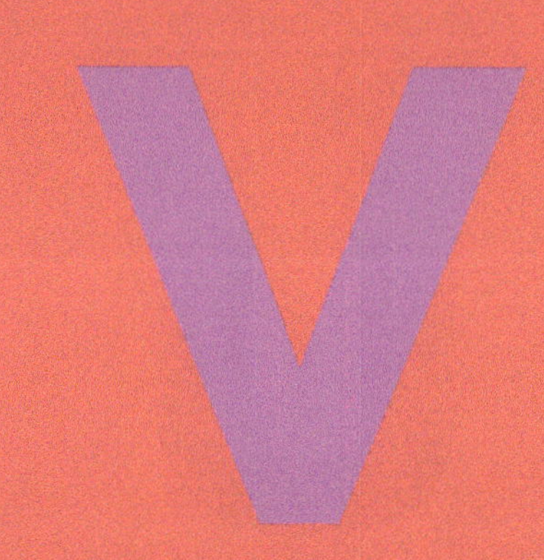

#DF134A

v is for violet cauliflower

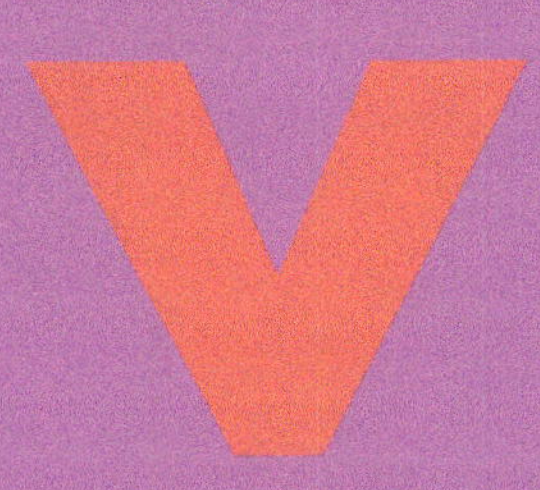

#C651B3

W is for watercress

W

#748C69

w is for wax bean

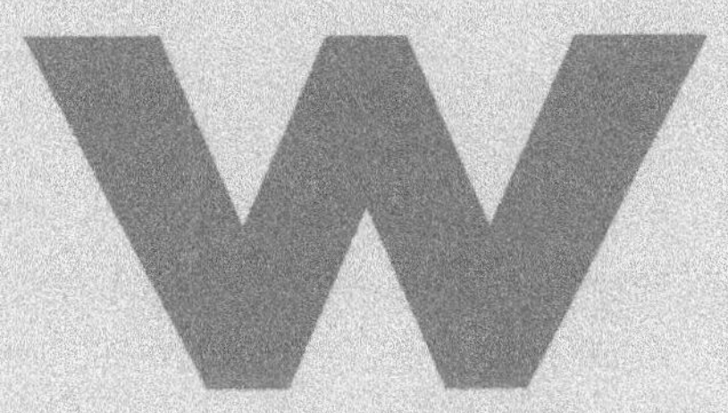

#E0C96B

X is for xanthosoma brasiliense

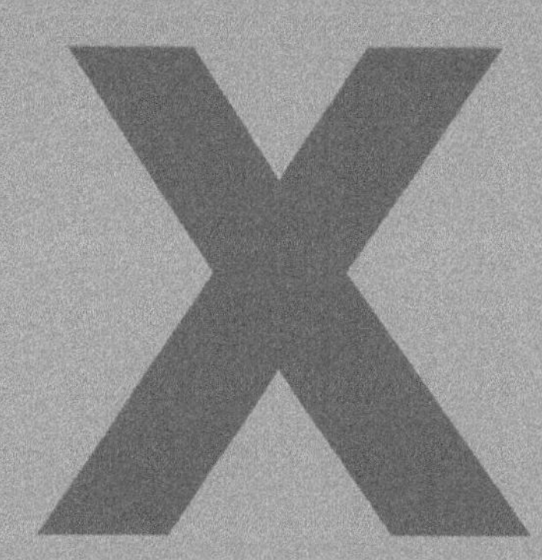

#709E4A

x is for xanthosoma sagittifolium

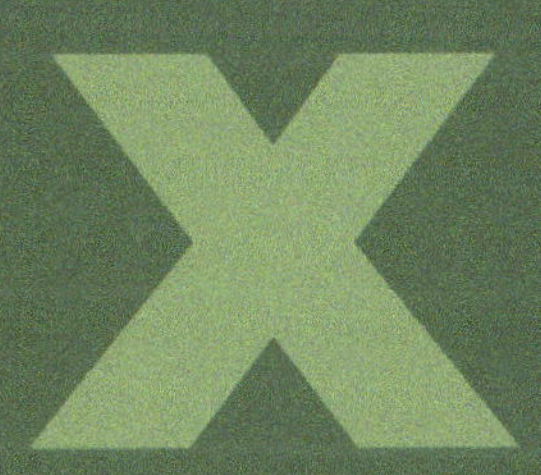

#035E1B

Y is for yacon

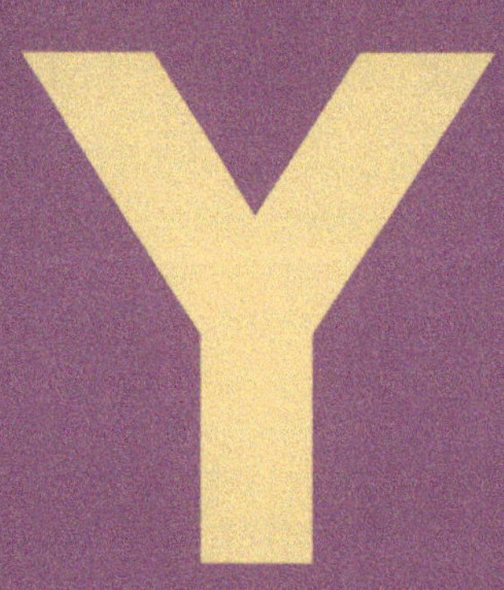

#A14D85

y is for yukon gold potato

y

#F3C775

Z is for zeller

Z

#E6CCCB

z is for zucchetta

z

#B3C86D